Your Body Belongs to You

Cornelia Spelman • illustrated by Teri Weidner

Albert Whitman & Company • Chicago, Illinois

Also by Cornelia Spelman:
Mama and Daddy Bear's Divorce
When I Care about Others
When I Feel Angry
When I Feel Good about Myself
When I Feel Jealous

When I Feel Sad
When I Feel Scared
When I Feel Worried
When I Miss You

Library of Congress Cataloging-in-Publication Data

Spelman, Cornelia.
Your body belongs to you/written by Cornelia Spelman; illustrated by Teri Weidner.
p. cm.
Summary: Explains what to say and do if someone touches your body when you do not want to be touched, especially when the action involves the touching of private parts.
1. Children and strangers—juvenile literature. 2. Child sexual abuse—juvenile literature.
[1. Child sexual abuse.] 1. Weidner, Teri, ill. 11 Title
HQ784.S8S74 1997
613.6—dc21 97—1787
CIP
AC

Text copyright © 1997 by Cornelia Spelman
Illustrations copyright © 1997 by Teri Weidner
Published in 1997 by Albert Whitman & Company
ISBN 978-0-8075-9473-5

Printed in China
33 32 31 30 29 28 LP 22 21 20 19 18 17

Designed by Scott Piehl

For more information about Albert Whitman & Company,
visit our website at www.albertwhitman.com.

For the children—CS

To Mr. Budd, my marvelous cat—TW

Note to Parents

Children need an abundance of warm physical affection to thrive. However, when children indicate that they don't want to be hugged or kissed, we need to respect their reactions. In this way, they learn that being touched is their own choice, not another's; that their bodies "belong to them."

We often unwittingly teach the opposite lesson when we force children to give a good-night kiss to a relative or friend or when we permit others to pick up, tickle, or kiss our children against their wishes.

There is a big difference, of course, between a friendly hug and sexual abuse. However, to protect our children against sexual abuse we must realize that abuse is only the most extreme end of a continuum of unwanted touch. Children who are taught very early that their bodies belong to them and that they have the right to decline touch are being taught that they are not powerless. They are being taught that their own response to touch counts.

This book is meant to convey a few simple ideas in simple language: a child's body is his or her own; a child has the right to decline touch—no matter how innocent; and the parts of a child's body covered by a bathing suit are never to be touched by others except in certain circumstances. Keeping the message simple is important for very young children.

Young children also need to know the words for the parts of their bodies, whether those are your special family words or the "correct" words. They need to know to tell you if anyone tries to touch their private parts.

Help them talk about what feels good and what feels bad (such as being tickled against their will). This leads to confidence in their own perceptions.

Explain to your children that *any* touching that has to be kept secret is not good touching. While there are pleasant secrets, such as not telling about a birthday present, secrets about touching are always suspicious and never permitted.

If your children tell you someone has touched them in ways that make them uneasy, pay close attention. Find out exactly what happened to cause their discomfort, and protect them from contact with the person involved while you figure out what's going on. Reassure them that it is right to talk about such things, that you take their discomfort seriously, and that you will keep them safe.

As your children mature, they'll give you many opportunities to teach them more. Let them know that you welcome any questions about any subject. Children who know that they can talk to their parents will have an ongoing source of protection from many possible dangers, including sexual abuse.

—Cornelia Spelman, ACSW, LCSW

Most of the time, you like to be
touched. It feels good to get a hug
or kiss.

You say, "I like that!" You hug and kiss back or snuggle closer.

Sometimes you don't like to be touched. Sometimes you don't want a hug or kiss, even from someone you love.

Then you can say, "No, not right now, please!" Or you can show you don't want to be touched by not hugging or kissing back or by pulling away.

Even if you don't want a hug or kiss right now, you can still be friends.

If someone still doesn't understand, ask your mom or dad or another grown-up to help you say, "No, not right now, please!" Your body belongs to you!

Some places on your body should never be touched by other people— except when you need help in the bathroom or getting dressed or when you go to the doctor.

These are the places on your body covered by a bathing suit. They are called your "private parts."

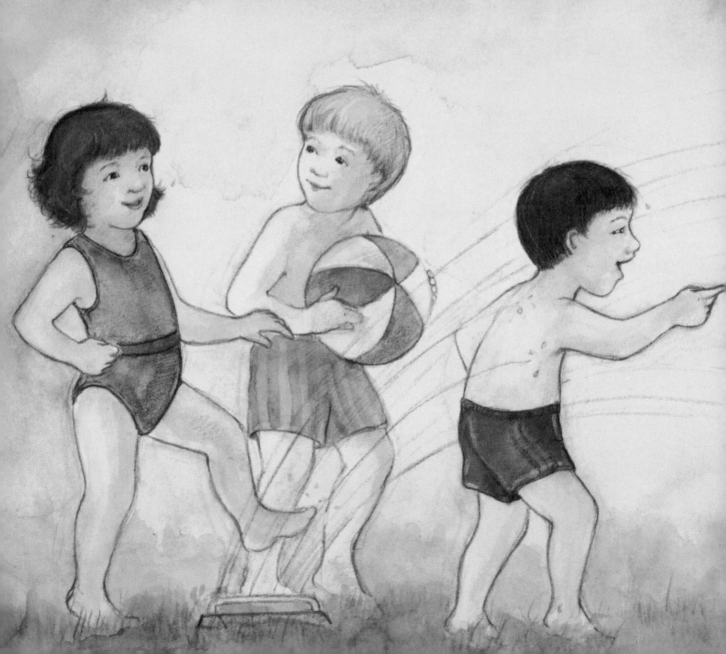

If anyone tries to touch your private parts, tell your parents or another grown-up you trust.

Your body belongs to you! When you don't want a hug or kiss, it's okay to say, "No, not right now, please!"

And it's important to tell if someone tries to touch your private parts.

Sometimes you like to be touched, and sometimes you don't. But mostly, getting a hug or kiss and being close to other people feels good.

You like that!